Fore

Affirmations have been around for a long time, but in the last couple of years it seems like a lightbulb has came in society concerning affirmations. Affirmations are positive ways of encouraging yourself with bold, confident, and positive words. Words are also creative forces, so to release words into the atmosphere gives them the freedom to create on your behalf.

Anitra has done an amazing job with delivering the simplicity of affirmations. Many people often have a hard time getting started with affirmations, but she has done a wonderful job with giving a blueprint to get started. These affirmations will empower and bless every person that reads them and speak them into the atmosphere.

Dr. Michelle McCormick

Faith comes by hearing!

Hearing comes by the

WORD OF GOD!

SEE IT

SPEAK IT

RECEIVE IT

into your mind, body, and spirit.

I LOVE JESUS

I accept Jesus as my Lord and
Savior.

The Blood of Jesus flows within
my
mind and reigns over my body &
spirit.

The Blood of Jesus covers and
protects me from all hurt and harm.

BECAUSE JESUS CAN'T FAIL,
I CAN'T FAIL

I have POWER and AUTHORITY
just like Jesus!

I AM LOVING ME JUST FOR ME

I AM HAPPY

I AM BEAUTIFUL

I AM CREATIVE

I AM FEARLESS

I AM RESILIENT

I AM A BORN LEADER

I AM A RESOURCEFUL

I AM A GREAT ACHIEVER

I AM A GREAT NURTURER

I AM A GREAT PERSON

MY FATHERS CHILD

I am a unique woman of God, I will
not compare myself to others
I am WORTHY of a wonderful,
successful happy life
I am NEVER alone
I am BLESSED
I am intelligent and well able to do
ANYTHING I set my mind to do!

I AM

LOVED

LOVING

SMART

STRONG

BEAUTIFUL

HONEST

CAPABLE

COURAGEOUS

WANTED BY GOD

NEEDED BY GOD

A VALUABLE ASSET

GOOD ENOUGH

I AM GOD'S CHILD

I am AWESOME

I am FORGIVING

I am HEALTHY

I am FEARLESS

I am GORGEOUS

I am CREATIVE

I am TALENTED

I am TRAIL-BLAZER

I am HONEST and TRUTHFUL

I am SMART and SUCCESSFUL

I have NO LIMITS TO MY LIFE

NO ONE is better than me!

I am created PERFECT by GOD just as I am! Whatever I do I ALWAYS give it my all!

ONLY GOD IS PERFECT

Everybody makes mistakes.

It's ok to ask for help and give

help to others if it doesn't hurt me.

I can say NO!

I don't have to agree with others;

or do I always have to share and

ive to other people.

I MATTER!

I HAVE A GOD GIVEN PURPOSE TO FULFILL

I AM IMPORTANT

What I have to say is important, I will not be afraid to speak up for myself.

I have a right to defend myself to ANYONE

I will NOT accept anyone mistreating

me because I matter!

I am worth being LOVED and RESPECTED!

I BELIEVE in God, so I BELIEVE in myself!

I WON'T GIVE UP

ON MYSELF

OR MY DREAMS

I ALWAYS WIN

BECAUSE

I ALWAYS

TRY MY BEST

GOD LOVES ME

I treat my body with respect and

make others!

I am valuable!

I am worth being respected!

I am worth being listened to!

I am worth being loved!

I am worth EVERYTHING God has

planned and destined for me!

I am accepted by God and those who

matter!

I am who the word of God says I am!

Noone else's opinion counts!

I AM CREATED

IN THE EXPRESS

IMAGE AND FAVOR

OF GOD AS

HIS VIRTUOUS WOMAN.

HE LOVES &

BELIEVES IN ME

AND

I LOVE

&

BELIEVE IN HIM !

I AM AWESOME
NO ONE
can tear me down
or make me feel bad
because
I don't
give them permission
or accept their lies.
I ONLY BELIEVE GOD !!

GOD FORGAVE ME

I forgive myself for my mistakes.
I forgive other people for their
mistakes that hurt me.
I give all hurt & pain to God.
All my problems have solutions.
NOTHING is too great for God !
My challenges help me to grow.
EVERYDAY I get better.

I AM ENOUGH!

THERE IS

NO ONE BETTER

THAN ME

I AM CONFIDENT

IN WHO I AM

I WILL

ALWAYS SUCCEED

I AM

THE BEST VERSION

OF ME

I AM A BRANCH OF THE VINE

I speak with FULL power and
authority just like Jesus Christ!
I am a woman of pure
EXCELLENCE!
I have full ability to learn, remember
and do EVERYTHING related to
work, my family, my purpose, the
word of God and anything in life!
I have discernment of good and evil.
I will not be tricked by the enemy
because I choose to ONLY obey God!

I AM
THE FAVOR
OF GOD.
I AM
A JOINT
HEIR WITH
JESUS CHRIST
I POSSESS HIS
FULL INHERITANCE
I AM RIGHTEOUS
ONCE I ACCEPT HIM !

I CAN DO

ALL THINGS...ANYTHING

I COULD EVER THINK

OR IMAGINE

THROUGH

JESUS CHRIST

WHO GIVES ME

ALL

ABILITY AND POWER!!!

Philippians 4:13

I AM

THE DAUGHTER

PRAYER WARRIOR

APPOINTED WOMAN

FULL OF GRACE

MERCY FORGIVENESS

STRATEGY & WISDOM

PREPARED

FOR SUCH A TIME

AS THIS TO BE

IMPACTFUL

IN MY DADDY'S

KINGDOM !

I HAVE FULL

ABILITY

SKILL

CREATIVITY

TRUST

RESOURCES

ACCESS

EVERYTHING

I NEED

TO ACCOMPLISH

ANYTHING

AND

GOD

EVERYTHING

I CHOOSE

BECAUSE GOD SAID SO !

think

I AM HEALED IN EVERY AREA OF OF MY

 -GOD

Thank You

Please visit:

anitrathames.com

Made in the USA
Columbia, SC
13 July 2024